THE SILENT LOAD

Men, Mental Health, and the Pressure to be Strong in Modern India

C.S. Activist

This book is intended for informational and educational purposes only. It is not a substitute for professional medical, psychological, or legal advice. Readers experiencing mental health difficulties should seek support from qualified professionals or appropriate support services.

Every effort has been made to ensure the accuracy of the information presented in this book. However, the author makes no representations or warranties regarding the completeness or suitability of the information for any particular purpose.

Names and identifying details in case examples have been changed where necessary to protect privacy.

First published in 2026.

Cover design by the author.

This book discusses mental health, suicide, and social stress affecting men. It is intended for educational and informational purposes only and is not a substitute for professional medical, psychological, or legal advice. If you or someone you know is in crisis, please seek support from qualified professionals or contact a mental health helpline listed in the Resources section.

Table of Contents

Introduction: The Quiet Weight

Across the world, a strange pattern repeats itself.

Men are less likely to visit a therapist. Less likely to speak openly about distress. Less likely to admit they are struggling. Yet they are far more likely to die by suicide.

In India, the gap is stark. According to the 2023 report from the National Crime Records Bureau, 73% of all suicide deaths in the country were men — a figure that holds across regions, income levels, professions, and social classes. Farmers, students, software engineers, small business owners, daily wage labourers, government employees — the data does not belong to a single group. It belongs to men in general.

73%

Male Suicide Share

of all suicide deaths in India — NCRB 2023, 171,418 total

Despite these numbers, men's mental health rarely occupies the centre of public discussion. When it appears, it is often framed indirectly — through addiction, violence, burnout, or economic stress. The emotional life beneath those behaviours remains largely invisible.

Part of the reason is cultural. Many societies have historically assigned men the roles of provider, protector, and problem-solver. These roles carry honour and responsibility, but they also contain an unspoken rule: the person carrying the load must not complain about its weight.

> *Strength, in this script, is defined as endurance. And endurance, when pushed past its limits without relief, becomes a crisis.*

The result is a paradox. Many men develop a remarkable capacity for perseverance, responsibility, and sacrifice. Yet the same qualities that make them dependable can also make them psychologically isolated. A man who believes his role is to solve problems alone may hesitate to admit when he himself is the problem that needs care.

This is what psychologists increasingly refer to as the silent load — the accumulation of pressures that remain largely unspoken: financial expectations, identity tied to work, relationship breakdown, social stigma around vulnerability, and the quiet loneliness that many men experience in adulthood.

Unlike dramatic crises, the silent load grows slowly. A stressful job. A difficult marriage. Debt. An aging parent who needs care. A child who needs school fees. A society that expects composure at all times. Individually, each pressure may seem manageable. Together, they can create a psychological landscape where distress builds quietly beneath the surface of everyday life.

The purpose of this book is not to claim that men suffer more than women. Human suffering cannot be measured like rainfall in competing cities. Rather, the argument is simpler and more precise: men often suffer differently. Their distress frequently appears not as tears or confession, but as irritability, withdrawal, risk-taking, addiction, or relentless overwork. These behaviours are often interpreted as personal flaws rather than signals of underlying psychological strain.

It is also worth stating clearly at the outset: recognizing men's mental health challenges does not diminish the very real struggles faced by women and girls. Gender equality is not a zero-sum equation. Societies can simultaneously address violence against women, workplace discrimination, and the silent psychological burdens carried by men. The purpose of this book is simply to illuminate one side of the mental health landscape that has historically received less attention — not to suggest that this side is the only one that matters.

Understanding this pattern requires looking beyond stereotypes. We must examine the interaction of biology, culture, identity, and modern economic pressures that shape how men experience stress — and how they are allowed to respond to it. Only then can we begin to answer a difficult question: why do so many men struggle silently, and what would it take to change that?

CHAPTER 1

The Man Who Could Not Speak

Case Study: Arjun's Story

Arjun was thirty-eight years old. He lived in Bengaluru and worked as a senior engineer at a multinational technology company. On paper, his life looked like a modest success story.

He had a stable salary. A two-bedroom apartment purchased through a long EMI. A wife and a six-year-old daughter. A car parked in the basement of a gated apartment complex. His parents often told relatives how proud they were of him.

Arjun himself rarely thought about whether he was happy.

Like many men, he measured life in terms of responsibilities rather than emotions. The important question was not 'How do I feel?' but 'What needs to be handled next?' Life moved forward through obligation, and for several years, this rhythm worked.

But slowly, something began to shift.

At first it appeared as irritability. Small frustrations at work triggered disproportionate anger. A delayed email response from a colleague felt like a personal insult. Meetings that once seemed routine began to feel exhausting. At home, he became quieter. His wife occasionally asked if something was wrong. 'Nothing,' he would reply — and he was not lying. He genuinely did not know what to say.

Because what he felt was not sadness in the way people imagine depression. He was not crying or expressing despair. Instead, he felt something harder to name: restlessness, fatigue, a low constant pressure behind his chest. Sleep gradually became irregular. Some nights he lay awake scrolling through his phone until two in the morning. Other nights he woke suddenly with his heart racing, as though he had forgotten something urgent.

At work he began staying longer hours — partly to escape the tension at home, partly because work at least provided structure.

Then one afternoon, after a difficult meeting with his manager, Arjun walked to the basement parking area and sat in his car. He did not start the engine. He simply sat there. For the first time in his life, he felt something close to panic. His chest felt tight. His palms were sweating. And a strange thought entered his mind: 'I don't want to go back upstairs.'

Nothing catastrophic had happened. He had not lost his job. His family was still intact. Yet something inside him had clearly reached a breaking point.

Male-Type Depression: Irritability, Overwork, and Withdrawal

Arjun's experience is not unusual. Psychologists increasingly recognize that men often experience depression differently from women. Traditional descriptions of depression emphasize sadness, crying, and emotional despair. But many men express distress through a different pattern — sometimes called male-type depression.

Instead of visible sadness, symptoms may include:

- irritability and a shortened temper
- compulsive overwork as avoidance
- emotional withdrawal from family life
- substance use or digital escapism
- increased risk-taking behaviour

The underlying emotional pain is real, but its expression does not fit common stereotypes of depression. As a result, many men fail to recognize their own condition. They assume they are simply stressed. Or tired. Or frustrated with work. And because they do not recognize the problem, they rarely seek help.

The Gender Paradox of Suicide

This creates one of the most striking statistical anomalies in public health: the gender paradox of suicide. Across most countries, women are diagnosed with depression and anxiety at higher rates than men. Yet men die by suicide at significantly higher rates. In India, that ratio is 73% male

The discrepancy is not coincidental. It is the predictable outcome of a system that only recognizes one face of distress — the tearful, openly suffering face — while missing the irritable, withdrawn, overworking face entirely. Men are suffering; they are simply suffering in ways that conventional diagnostic frameworks are not calibrated to catch.

> *The diagnostic gap — women recorded as struggling, men dying from their struggle — is not a statistical accident. It is the gap created when emotional pain has only one acceptable shape.*

Understanding this paradox requires examining the cultural expectations that shape how men experience and express emotion. Those expectations begin long before adulthood. They begin in childhood.

CHAPTER 2

The Architecture of Silence

Emotional Socialization: 'Boys Don't Cry'

Consider a simple childhood moment. A young boy falls while playing and begins to cry. Before the tears fully appear, someone nearby often says: 'Don't cry. Be a man.'

The sentence may be spoken casually, even affectionately. But its psychological meaning is powerful. It tells the child that emotional expression is incompatible with masculinity. From that moment forward, certain feelings — fear, sadness, helplessness — become difficult to display. The child learns to hide them.

Psychologists refer to this process as emotional socialization: the way children gradually learn which emotional expressions are acceptable within their culture. In the Indian household, this socialization is often expressed through specific linguistic commands:

- Chot nahi lagi (You aren't hurt)
- Ladke rote nahi hain (Boys don't cry)
- Bahadur bano (Be brave)

Over time, these messages coalesce into a cultural script. The boy learns not simply to stop crying but to stop registering certain emotions altogether. The internal alarm system begins to be dismantled — not by external force, but by internal compliance.

The Social Contract of Masculinity: Status for Sacrifice

For much of human history, male roles involved significant risk — warfare, hunting, and physically demanding labour. In return for accepting these risks, societies granted men authority and status. Some researchers describe this arrangement as a form of social exchange: society rewarded male sacrifice while expecting emotional resilience in return.

Seager, Farrell, and Barry (2016) describe this as the archetypal male gender script — an evolutionary and near-universal pressure defining how men must live to be considered successful. It consists of three core rules:

1. Be a fighter and a winner
2. Be a provider and a protector
3. Retain mastery and control over feelings

This script was not designed to harm men. It evolved to protect social groups through male sacrifice. But over centuries, what began as a social arrangement has hardened into a psychological rule: men should handle problems alone.

The consequences are subtle but profound. Human emotions do not disappear simply because they are discouraged. When feelings are suppressed repeatedly, they tend to reappear through indirect channels: anger, irritability, physical tension, chronic fatigue, sleep disturbance.

> *Rather than simply expecting men to talk differently, we need to learn to listen differently to them — and to recognize that emotional expression in men may look like withdrawal, overwork, or irritability rather than tears.*

Psychological research shows that emotional suppression increases physiological stress responses. Heart rate and blood pressure rise, and stress hormones remain chronically elevated. Over time, the body begins carrying what we call the silent load.

CHAPTER 3

The Physiology of Suppressed Pain

The Amygdala and the Science of Labelling Emotions

Most people imagine emotional suffering as something purely psychological — a storm of thoughts or feelings inside the mind. But the mind does not float somewhere outside the body. Emotion is biology. Every emotional experience is accompanied by changes in the nervous system, hormones, muscles, breathing, and heart rate. When distress persists for long periods, these physiological systems begin carrying the burden.

For many men, this is how psychological strain first appears — not as tears or confession, but as physical discomfort: chest tightness, acid reflux, back pain, headaches, chronic fatigue, insomnia.

The brain is equipped with a survival mechanism called the amygdala. When we encounter stress — whether it is a looming deadline, a difficult conversation at home, or a financial threat — the amygdala triggers the fight-or-flight response. The body mobilizes. Adrenaline increases. Cortisol rises. The heart pumps faster. Breathing becomes shallow.

In short bursts, this response is useful. It prepares the body to handle danger. But when the stress response is activated repeatedly over months or years without resolution, the system stops resetting itself.

A landmark study by Lieberman et al. (2007) demonstrated something remarkable: simply putting feelings into words — affect labeling — reduces activity in the amygdala and increases activity in the prefrontal cortex, the region responsible for reasoning and emotional regulation. In other words, naming an emotion helps calm the nervous system.

↓ Amygdala

The Affect Labeling Effect

Naming an emotion reduces brain alarm-system activity (Lieberman et al., 2007)

But for men who have been socially conditioned never to name feelings, this regulatory mechanism becomes inaccessible. The emotion remains active within the nervous system. The amygdala stays in a state of chronic hyper-arousal. Over time, the body absorbs the load.

Somatic Manifestations: From Headaches to Heart Strain

A feeling that cannot become a sentence often becomes a symptom.

Common physical manifestations of suppressed emotional stress in men include:

- **Chest tightness:** frequently mistaken for cardiac issues, often the result of chronic anxiety and bracing of the intercostal muscles
- **Gastrointestinal distress:** through the gut-brain axis, which is highly sensitive to sustained cortisol elevation
- **Musculoskeletal tension:** in the jaw (bruxism), neck, and lower back — the body's literal armour against perceived threat
- **Sleep fragmentation:** waking at 3–4 a.m. with a racing heart — a classic sign of a nocturnal cortisol spike

When the alarm system never turns off, chronic exposure to cortisol and adrenaline leads to systemic inflammation, increased cardiovascular risk, and neuroplastic changes — the hippocampus (responsible for memory and emotional regulation) can physically shrink under prolonged stress, making the person more reactive and less able to handle future challenges.

Because vulnerability is stigmatized, men often convert their fear or sadness into anger. From a physiological standpoint, anger feels active and strong, whereas sadness feels passive and weak. This conversion is a survival strategy — but it keeps heart rate high and blood pressure elevated, further taxing the cardiovascular system.

> *Understanding that mental health is physical health is the first step toward resilience. A man who learns to label his stress isn't becoming 'emotional' — he is manually lowering his blood pressure and protecting his long-term health.*

Many men encounter their emotional life indirectly, through physical signals. They notice that they cannot sleep. They develop unexplained digestive problems. They feel constantly restless or irritated. Because these symptoms appear physical, they often seek purely medical solutions — painkillers for headaches, antacids for stomach discomfort, alcohol for sleep. These interventions provide temporary relief but do not address the underlying emotional strain.

The Biology of Male Stress: Why the Body Responds Differently

It is worth being precise about what is biological and what is cultural in men's stress experience — because both matter, and conflating them leads to confusion.

At the biological level, several mechanisms shape how men's bodies respond to stress differently from women's. The hypothalamic-pituitary-adrenal axis — the body's central stress response system — triggers higher and more sustained cortisol release in men under acute stress, priming a stronger fight-or-flight response. This is adaptive in short bursts but becomes damaging when stress is chronic and unresolved.

Some research suggests that women's stress responses more often involve oxytocin-mediated social bonding pathways — sometimes called the 'tend-and-befriend' response — the impulse to seek social connection and mutual support when under threat. While the evidence is complex and context-dependent, this line of research suggests that for many men, the biological pull under stress leans more strongly toward isolation and action than toward social approach. Oxytocin plays a role in calming emotions and enabling bonding, and individual differences in these pathways may partly explain why social support-seeking feels less instinctively accessible to many men under pressure.

Additionally, chronic stress suppresses testosterone production. This is relevant because lowered testosterone is associated with increased pain perception — a finding that helps explain why men under prolonged psychological stress often present with heightened physical sensitivity and somatic complaints, even when the root cause is emotional.

> *Men's stress response is not simply a weaker version of the same system. It is a differently calibrated system — one that was shaped for short-term physical threat, not for the sustained, invisible, relational pressures of modern life.*

This biological context does not excuse emotional suppression or make it inevitable. Culture amplifies what biology initiates. But understanding the biological substrate helps explain why many men genuinely find social support-seeking less instinctively accessible than women do — and why the toolkit for men must include explicit skills for connection and regulation that women may acquire more naturally through the tend-and-befriend pathway.

The Help-Seeking Gap: What the Numbers Reveal

The biological and cultural forces described in this chapter converge on a stark outcome: men use mental health services at dramatically lower rates than women. According to NIMHANS data from 2022, only approximately 20% of mental health service users in India are male — despite men comprising 73% of suicide completions (NCRB, 2023).

This gap is not evidence that men suffer less. It is evidence that the barriers between suffering and help are substantially higher for men than for women. Those barriers are simultaneously biological (stress response differences and the reduced tend-and-befriend pathway), psychological (identity armour and stoicism), cultural (the three-rule masculine script), and structural (the scarcity of male-appropriate mental health services and the gender blindness of many existing providers).

In a country with just 0.3 psychiatrists per 100,000 people (WHO, 2023), the mental health system is already stretched beyond capacity. When the small pool of available support is further underutilised by men — the very group dying at highest rates from psychological distress — the result is a silent crisis that conventional health metrics consistently fail to capture.

CHAPTER 4

The Provider Trap & Identity Fusion

Identity Fusion: When Self-Worth Equals Net Worth

In India, the male identity is often built on a single, precarious foundation: the role of the provider. When a man's entire sense of self is fused with his economic utility, any threat to his career or financial stability becomes an existential threat to his life. This is identity fusion, and in the high-pressure landscape of modern India, it is a primary driver of the silent load.

Despite the rise of dual-income households, the cultural expectation in many Indian families remains that the man is the ultimate financial safety net. This manifests as a relentless cycle of obligations:

- **The EMI cycle:** a 20-year home loan that feels like a tether to a job he may quietly despise

- **Parental dependency:** the expectation to fund medical care and retirement for aging parents

- **The marriage market:** in many circles, a man's social worth is indexed directly to his CTC (Cost to Company)

- **Children's futures:** education, healthcare, and housing as long-term psychological commitments

Psychologists use the term identity fusion to describe a state where the boundaries between the self and a role disappear. A healthy identity is like a house with many rooms: I am a father, a runner, a friend, and an engineer. If one room catches fire — say, a job loss — the rest of the house remains standing. A fused identity is a single-room studio apartment. If the career fails, the man feels there is nothing left of him.

This fusion explains why NCRB data consistently shows elevated male suicide rates during economic downturns or after professional setbacks. To the fused man, a layoff isn't a temporary setback; it is an identity collapse.

Case Reflection: When Systems Become Stress Multipliers — The Atul Subhash Case

In December 2024, Atul Subhash, a 34-year-old artificial intelligence engineer based in Bengaluru, died by suicide. He left behind a 24-page written account and an 81-minute video detailing what he described as a prolonged and compounding ordeal: a contested marriage, allegations of harassment from in-laws, protracted legal proceedings, and the denial of meaningful contact with his four-year-old son.

His case became one of the most widely discussed public conversations about male mental health in India in recent memory. It is referenced here not to adjudicate its legal dimensions, which remain contested, but to examine the psychological architecture his account describes — because it maps almost precisely onto the framework of this chapter.

Provider pressure: Atul was, by every external measure, a successful provider. He had built a career in a high-demand field. Yet his account suggests that this success afforded him no psychological protection when his identity as a father and partner was threatened.

Legal stress as an amplifier: The experience of prolonged legal proceedings — regardless of their merits — creates a distinct form of chronic stress. It combines unpredictability, public exposure, financial drain, and a profound sense of powerlessness. For men whose sense of competence is central to their identity, the experience of feeling unable to resolve a situation through effort can be particularly destabilising.

Institutional helplessness: His account describes repeated encounters with systems — courts, police, administrative processes — that felt unresponsive or inaccessible. This experience of institutional helplessness is documented as a significant psychological risk factor, particularly when combined with social isolation and shame.

Identity collapse: Perhaps most tellingly, his final communications describe a man who had not lost his ability to articulate his experience — he was remarkably precise and detailed. What he appears to have lost was any sense of a pathway forward. The fused identity — father, provider, engineer, husband — had been dismantled systematically, and no psychological floor remained.

The Atul Subhash case illustrates what this book terms the silent load at its most extreme: not a sudden crisis but an accumulation of pressures — relational, legal, financial, and existential — that the man carried largely alone, in the belief that carrying them was his obligation. The tragedy is not only personal. It is a mirror held up to a system of social and psychological expectations that needs to change.

The Empathy Gap and Male Gender Blindness

Compounding this is a phenomenon researchers call the gender empathy gap — a societal tendency to be less attuned to or responsive to the suffering of men compared to women and children.

Research by Seager, Farrell, and Barry (2016) argues that this gap has evolutionary roots. Some evolutionary psychologists suggest that societies historically relied on men to undertake higher-risk roles — warfare, dangerous labour, physical protection — which may have shaped cultural expectations around male sacrifice and self-sufficiency. As a result, a man in trouble may evoke less instinctive sympathy than a woman or child in equivalent distress.

In the workplace, this empathy gap is particularly visible. Men are often viewed through the lens of utility. A man who is struggling is frequently told to 'buckle down' or 'man up.' Admitting to burnout is perceived in many corporate cultures as a lack of leadership potential. Men are socialized to compete rather than to collaborate on emotional well-being, creating a 'lonely at the top' dynamic — and, crucially, also a 'lonely in the middle and at the bottom' dynamic.

> *When it comes to gender equality we tend to only think of women as having legitimate cause for complaint. But the silent toll of male suffering — in suicides, workplace deaths, homelessness — demands the same moral seriousness.*

Male Disposability: The Economics of Expendability

Embedded within the empathy gap is a deeper social logic that researchers call male disposability — the historical and structural tendency for societies to treat men's bodies and lives as expendable resources in service of collective goals.

The data on this is consistent across cultures and time periods. In India today, men account for over 90% of workplace fatalities (ILO, 2023), 95% of the prison population (NCRB, 2022), and over 73% of suicides (NCRB, 2023). Globally, men comprise the overwhelming majority of those killed in wars, industrial accidents, and dangerous occupations. These are not incidental statistics. They reflect a structural arrangement in which male lives are implicitly valued primarily for their productive and protective output.

This is not framed here as a grievance or a competition with women's suffering — which is real and extensively documented. It is framed as a diagnostic observation: when men internalize the message that their worth is conditional on what they produce and protect, they become psychologically reluctant to acknowledge their own distress. The disposable man does not take sick leave. He does not see a therapist. He does not disclose vulnerability. Because somewhere, encoded in the rules he received, is the lesson that admitting need makes him less eligible for the social contract.

Understanding male disposability is therefore not a political argument — it is a clinical tool. When a man struggles to justify seeking help, when he says 'I shouldn't complain, others have it worse', or 'I just need to push through', he is often enacting the disposability logic: minimizing his own suffering in deference to the expectation that he be useful rather than honest.

The solution is not to abandon responsibility or ambition. Work and contribution remain important sources of meaning. The challenge is to prevent identity from becoming so narrow that a single setback feels like the end of the self. A psychologically healthy identity must be broader than any single role.

Identity Armour: When Strength Becomes a Blind Spot

There is a paradox at the heart of the high-functioning man. The very qualities that make him effective — confidence, resilience, independence, a powerful sense of 'I'll be fine' — can become a psychological blind spot that masks declining health until the damage is severe.

Psychologists sometimes call this identity armour: the protective layer of self-sufficiency that a man builds up over decades of navigating difficulty alone. When young, this armour serves him well. It helps him push through setbacks, meet obligations, and project the composure his roles demand. But armour is rigid. It does not adapt to signals from inside.

A man wearing identity armour interprets fatigue as a reason to work harder. He interprets anxiety as weakness to be suppressed. He interprets his body's distress signals — the chest tightness, the disrupted sleep, the persistent irritability — as temporary inconveniences rather than information worth attending to. The armour that once protected him now prevents him from receiving care, from others and from himself.

> *Bottling up emotions — especially a tendency among South Asian and Indian men — has been repeatedly shown to increase the risk of heart disease and cancer. The armour that keeps distress invisible also keeps recovery out of reach.*

This is why identity armour is especially dangerous in the context of the silent load. The man who is most stoic, most apparently capable, most resistant to help is often the man whose internal load has reached the most critical point. The absence of visible struggle is not evidence of well-being. It is often evidence of exceptionally effective suppression.

Recognizing identity armour is therefore not an invitation to abandon strength. It is an invitation to update the definition of strength — to include the intelligence to know when the armour needs to come off, when self-assessment is a leadership skill rather than a weakness, and when seeking support is the most strategically sound decision a high-performing man can make.

CHAPTER 5

Coping by Substitution

When Emotional Expression Is Not Permitted

When emotional distress cannot be expressed directly, people often discover indirect ways to regulate their internal state. Psychologists sometimes refer to these as coping substitutions — attempts to manage emotional discomfort without confronting its source.

For many men, these substitutions follow familiar patterns: working longer hours, drinking alcohol, watching pornography, immersing themselves in video games or online content, taking physical risks. From the outside, these behaviours may appear unrelated. But they share a common psychological function: they alter the brain's reward chemistry.

At the centre of this system lies dopamine — a neurotransmitter involved in motivation, reward, and anticipation. When an activity produces a dopamine surge, the brain temporarily experiences relief from stress. Work achievement, sexual stimulation, alcohol and drugs, video games and social media — each offers a brief psychological escape. For someone carrying the silent load, that escape can feel essential.

The Numbing Hierarchy

In the Indian context, coping substitutions generally fall into three categories, often shaped by social class and professional context:

1. **Workaholism (the 'socially acceptable' addiction):** For many men, the office is the only place where they feel a sense of agency. When home life feels overwhelming or internal thoughts become too loud, they sink into work. This is rarely about productivity — it is about using professional tasks as a barrier against self-reflection. Workaholism is socially rewarded, making it uniquely dangerous as a

coping mechanism.

2. **Digital numbing:** With India having some of the cheapest mobile data rates in the world, smartphones have become primary tools for emotional regulation. High-stimulation content — short-form videos, gaming, pornography — triggers dopamine releases that temporarily drown out the cortisol of daily stress. But tolerance develops rapidly.
3. **Chemical substitution:** The use of alcohol or tobacco as a 'winding down' ritual. In many male circles, 'having a drink' is the only socially sanctioned way to lower one's guard — yet it frequently becomes a physiological dependency that further destabilizes the nervous system.

The Five Dimensions of Behavioural Addiction

How can someone distinguish a healthy coping strategy from a substitution that has become entrenched? Psychologists look for five markers:

- **Salience:** the activity dominates your thoughts even when you aren't doing it

- **Mood modification:** you use it specifically to escape uncomfortable feelings

- **Tolerance:** you need more of the activity — more hours, more intensity — to achieve the same relief

- **Withdrawal:** you feel irritable, anxious, or unsettled when you cannot access it

- **Conflict:** it is beginning to interfere with your health, sleep, or relationships

Substitution is a survival strategy that eventually becomes a prison. It offers the relief of silence without the healing of peace. The path forward is not from noise to more noise, but from numbing to processing.

Many men believe that as long as they keep moving forward — paying the bills, attending the meetings — they are okay. They treat their substitutions as fuel to keep the engine running. The danger is that substitution acts like a local anaesthetic: it numbs the pain while the wound continues to fester. Eventually, the silent load becomes too heavy for even the strongest distraction to mask.

CHAPTER 6

The Toolkit for Mental Fitness

Three Pillars of Male Resilience

Men don't necessarily need to become different people. They need a broader psychological range. Strength, in the modern era, is defined by adaptive flexibility — the ability to shift from stoic resolve to emotional literacy when the situation demands it.

Crucially, the most effective interventions for men often work with the grain of masculine values rather than against them. Framing support as performance optimization, skill-building, or taking control significantly reduces stigma and increases engagement. Research by Ellis et al. (2013) found that young men are more likely to engage with programmes promoting 'mental fitness' and 'self-mastery' than those framing support in traditional mental health terms.

Pillar 1: Neurological Optimization — Regulation and Self-Compassion

Many men have been trained in emotional suppression, which actually increases physiological strain. The evidence-based alternative is emotional regulation: feeling, naming, and responding intelligently.

- **Label to Disable:** simply saying 'I feel undervalued' or 'I feel overwhelmed' reduces amygdala activation and engages the prefrontal cortex (Lieberman et al., 2007). It calms the brain's alarm system without requiring lengthy emotional discussion

- **The science of self-compassion:** often misunderstood as self-pity, self-compassion is a neurobiological off-switch for the threat system. While self-criticism spikes cortisol, asking 'What would I tell a friend in this situation?' activates the brain's safety circuitry (Neff, 2003)

- **Box breathing (4-4-4-4):** inhale for four counts, hold for four, exhale for four, hold for four. This manually activates the parasympathetic nervous system, reducing sympathetic arousal within minutes

- **The two-minute daily check-in:** before reaching for a phone or screen in the morning, pause and locate stress in the body. Name it. This small act of labelling begins the regulatory process

Pillar 2: Cognitive Agency — Flexibility and Hardiness

Rigid internal rules — 'I must never show weakness,' 'Failure defines me' — are the primary drivers of burnout. Cognitive flexibility, a cornerstone of CBT, involves identifying and updating these mental scripts.

- **Developing hardiness:** based on Kobasa's (1979) Hardiness Theory, resilient individuals view stress as a challenge rather than a threat. The shift from 'I am failing' to 'I am navigating a difficult moment' preserves identity during setbacks

- **The accomplishment audit:** combat learned helplessness by tracking small wins. A weekly list of three tasks completed and one problem handled well recalibrates the brain toward agency (Bandura, 1997)

- **Reframing help-seeking:** present the act of seeking help as taking control, not losing it. 'If you seek help, you are facing the problem and showing strength' — this goes with the grain of the masculinity script rather than against it

Pillar 3: Structural Support — Connection and Professional Growth

Social isolation is now recognised as one of the most significant mortality risks in modern medicine. Research by Holt-Lunstad et al. (2010) found that social isolation increases mortality risk by approximately 29% — a risk comparable to smoking 15 cigarettes per day. Men are disproportionately vulnerable to this risk: they have smaller social networks than women on average, are less likely to maintain friendships through life transitions, and are more likely to lose their primary social infrastructure through workplace exit, divorce, or relocation.

- **Low-friction socializing:** men don't need twenty friends; they need two reliable connections. Shared activities — sports, projects, professional mentorship — provide a context that makes emotional safety possible without requiring explicit emotional discussion

- **Reframing therapy as performance optimization:** men who view professional support as a skill-building exercise, analogous to the way athletes use sports psychologists, are significantly more likely to engage with it

- **Behavioural activation:** Jacobsen et al. (2001) propose using everyday activities to improve mental health. Physical movement, structure, and achievable goals can restore a sense of agency during depressive episodes

Five Additional Coping Domains

Beyond the three pillars, research on resilience identifies five further capacities that are particularly relevant for men navigating the silent load. These are not techniques but orientations — stable psychological stances that buffer against breakdown:

- **Optimism:** not naïve positivity, but a general expectation that good things remain possible and that current difficulties are temporary rather than permanent. Research consistently shows that optimism predicts better health outcomes, faster recovery from setbacks, and greater persistence. For men socialized to catastrophize in private while projecting confidence in public, developing genuine (evidence-based) optimism about their own capacity to navigate difficulty is a significant psychological asset

- **Moral compass and values clarity:** a clear sense of what matters and why — guiding decisions under pressure without requiring external validation. Men who have articulated their core values tend to navigate ambiguity and ethical complexity more effectively, experiencing less of the cognitive dissonance that arises when behavior and values misalign. Knowing what you stand for reduces the psychological cost of difficult choices

- **Self-awareness and insight:** awareness of one's internal state, thoughts, and emotional patterns. This is the meta-skill that makes all other coping possible: a man who cannot observe his own reactions cannot regulate them. Developing self-awareness does not require extensive therapy — a daily two-minute reflection on what you noticed about your own responses is sufficient to begin building this capacity

- **Hope:** distinct from optimism, hope involves both the belief that a goal is achievable and the perceived capacity to find pathways toward it. Men in crisis often retain the goal but lose the sense of pathway — they can see what they want but cannot imagine how to reach it. Building hope means identifying even one small concrete step, which restores a sense of agency that despair has collapsed

- **Tolerance of uncertainty:** the ability to function effectively amidst ambiguity and unpredictability without requiring resolution before acting. This is particularly relevant for men who tie their sense of control to external outcomes — financial results, career trajectories, relationships — all of which are inherently uncertain. Developing tolerance of uncertainty means learning to act with intention while accepting that outcomes are only partially within one's control

The Weekly Mental Fitness Audit

The following five-point check-in — grounded in the three pillars above — can serve as an early warning system. One minute, once a week:

1. **Physical:** have I moved my body or practised box-breathing to lower my cortisol this week?
2. **Cognitive:** have I identified one stressor and created a control-based response to it?
3. **Social:** have I engaged in a side-by-side activity with a friend or family member?
4. **Language:** have I labelled a difficult emotion this week instead of numbing it?
5. **Identity:** have I spent time on a hobby or interest that has zero financial utility?

CHAPTER 7

Masculinity Types and What Actually Works

Understanding Different Forms of Masculinity

Masculinity is not a monolith. Research in gender studies identifies several distinct forms, each with different implications for mental health outcomes:

1. Hegemonic masculinity: the stoic, dominant, and competitive ideal. Associated with strong social expectations of emotional suppression and self-reliance.
2. Subordinate or caring masculinity: more emotionally expressive and relational, with an emphasis on feelings and a caring ethos toward others. Often socially penalized in traditional contexts, yet associated with better mental health outcomes.
3. Marginal masculinity: shaped by caste, social class, and structural disadvantage. Men in marginal positions face additional pressures around status and respect that can intensify traditional masculine performance as a form of social survival. In India, caste intersects with masculinity in ways that significantly affect how men experience and respond to stress.
4. Complacent masculinity: the man who accepts the privileges of hegemonic masculinity without actively enforcing it — implicitly treated as the authority figure in any room he walks into, simply by being male. Complacent masculinity benefits from the system without interrogating it.
5. Protest masculinity: exaggerated hypermasculinity, often a psychological response to feeling marginalized or powerless. Associated with higher-risk behaviours and greater resistance to help-seeking.
6. Hybrid masculinity: a blend of traditional strength and modern emotional awareness. Increasingly common among younger, urban, educated generations. More psychologically flexible and associated with better outcomes.

The problem is not masculinity itself — it is rigidity. When a man believes he must be stoic to be a man, his mental health suffers. When he becomes psychologically flexible, his resilience increases substantially.

Beta Bias and Gender-Responsive Practice

Research with life coaches and psychotherapists reveals a phenomenon called beta bias — the tendency to minimize or overlook genuine gender differences in treatment preferences (Hare-Mustin & Marecek, 1988). Russ et al. (2015) found that while 90% of coaches reported that men and women had different needs, many simultaneously expressed reluctance to act on those differences for fear of stereotyping.

This creates a practical problem: if therapists treat men and women identically despite observed differences, they may fail to engage men effectively. Men, according to the coaches interviewed, are more likely to:

- seek help in response to 'big triggers' such as a health scare or major relationship breakdown, rather than gradual distress

- respond better to action-oriented, goal-focused framing rather than open-ended emotional exploration

- engage more readily when the coach or therapist uses language of competence, skill-building, and agency

- need explicit permission to express emotions within therapeutic settings

A gender-responsive approach — one that acknowledges average differences in communication styles while avoiding biological determinism — appears most empirically grounded. It is not about treating all men the same, but about being open to the possibility that the entry points, language, and structure of support may need to differ.

> *It is of greater ethical importance to recognize gender differences in talking therapies than to ignore them out of fear of stereotyping. The*

failure to adapt can deprive both men and women of the support that best meets their needs.

The Gendered Approaches Spectrum

A useful framework for thinking about how any programme, policy, or therapeutic relationship handles gender is the gendered approaches spectrum — a continuum from actively harmful to genuinely transformative:

- **Discriminatory:** reinforces harmful gender norms and actively causes harm. Examples include telling a man who discloses distress to 'toughen up', or designing mental health programmes that assume male stoicism is a character flaw to be corrected rather than a learned behaviour to be understood

- **Blind:** ignores gender differences entirely, treating men and women as having identical needs and identical starting points. Well-intentioned but often ineffective for men, as it fails to account for the different ways men experience and express distress

- **Sensitive:** recognizes that men and women have different needs and acknowledges gender power dynamics, but does not necessarily take specific action to address them. A step forward, but insufficient on its own

- **Responsive:** includes specific design choices and language adaptations to actively reduce the barriers men face in engaging with mental health support. Action-oriented framing, side-by-side models, and coaching language are examples of gender-responsive practice

- **Transformative:** designed around a fundamental aim of addressing root causes of gender norms within society. Transformative approaches seek to change the cultural expectations that make the silent load possible in the first place — through education, community norms, and systemic change

Most current mental health provision in India sits at the Blind or Sensitive end of this spectrum. The goal is not simply to move individuals from suffering to coping, but to build services, workplaces, and communities that progressively move toward the Responsive and Transformative end — where the conditions that create the silent load are themselves addressed.

Practical Implications: Coaching, Language, and the Fix-It Frame

The research by Russ et al. (2015) and Seager et al. (2016) converges on several practical principles for helping men engage with mental health support:

- **Use coaching framing, not therapy framing:** men respond significantly better to 'performance optimization' and 'skill-building' than to language implying something is broken. In the Indian context, a man who would never tell his friends he is seeing a therapist will often engage with a 'stress management consultant' or 'performance coach'

- **Leverage the fix-it instinct:** rather than asking a man to stop trying to fix the problem and simply feel the emotion, skilled practitioners frame emotions as data and psychological support as a debugging process. The emotional work follows from the practical engagement

- **Use the side-by-side model:** men often bond and open up during shared activity — walking, driving, working on a task — rather than face-to-face sitting. Reducing the pressure of direct eye contact can lower defences significantly

- **Invoke generativity as the hook:** men are often strongly motivated by the need to be useful to others. Framing mental health support as necessary for the mission — 'you need to be well so you can be present for your family' — activates engagement where purely self-focused appeals do not

CHAPTER 8

The Male Life Cycle

Pressure Across the Decades

The silent load is not a static weight. It is a shifting burden that evolves through predictable stages. In India, a man's mental health is often tied to his perceived utility — his ability to provide, protect, and perform. When that utility is threatened or withdrawn, the risk of identity collapse spikes. Understanding the life cycle reveals where and how the accumulation happens.

The Performance Phase: Ages 16–25

The transition to manhood in India is marked by high-stakes competition. From board exams to engineering and medical entrances, the young man's worth becomes indexed to a rank. The failure stigma at this stage is acute: research into the gender empathy gap shows that society offers less emotional cushioning to young men who do not perform. A young man who 'fails' an exam often feels he has lost his place in the social hierarchy before his adult life has even begun.

This is also where the architecture of silence is most actively reinforced. To show stress is seen as a lack of grit. Many young men leaving home for studies or work experience a profound narrowing of social support, and emotional isolation can set in quickly. NCRB data shows that the 18–30 age group constitutes one of the two largest groups among suicide deaths in India.

The Provider Peak: Ages 26–55

This is the Arjun phase — the period of maximum identity fusion. The man is now the central pillar for his parents, his spouse, and his children. The EMI treadmill, the pressure of the home loan, school fees, and parental medical care creates a state of chronic sympathetic nervous system activation.

This is also the period when the invisibility of the provider is most dangerous. As noted by Seager et al. (2016), the provider is often viewed as a utility rather